# Let it Rain
## Inspirational Writings

By

Rev. Christopher S. Times

This book is a work of fiction. Places, events, and situations in this story are purely fictional. Any resemblance to actual persons, living or dead, is coincidental.

© 2002 by Rev. Christopher S. Times. All rights reserved.

No part of this book may be reproduced, stored in a retrieval system, or transmitted by any means, electronic, mechanical, photocopying, recording, or otherwise, without written permission from the author.

ISBN: 1-4033-9737-6 (softcover)
ISBN: 1-4033-9736-8 (electronic)

This book is printed on acid free paper.

1st Books - rev. 12/18/02

# Dedication

I dedicate this book to my wonderful parents Roy and Jean Times, and to my family and dear friends who encouraged and refused to let me give up my desire. Thank you!

Lest I not forget my fine children; Jessica, Louis Demond and Lucy, you are wonderful and so very special to me. I love you.

# Forward

I am persuaded by the Gospel of Jesus Christ, that we are living in perilous and desperate times. As a direct result, the "historical" family is being destroyed through conventional means...it stands on unstable ground. I contend that this fabric of American society, in the wake of such devices as domestic and family violence, is perpetuating a self-seeking end to a once and still Holy doctrine...that of marriage and family. It is true, that the world is but a mirror unto itself, reflecting it's own selfish and temporal desires, wishes, and needs. It is this vain of destructive thought that helps enable the "crippling process" of Let's Destroy America. It's the thought of evil for evil and deception for deception which propels us to an unending cycle of violence, one to another. The fabric of this society has dwindled to a cheap version of "Let's make a deal", featuring ourselves as targets to relentless violence as rape, murder, kidnapping, all kinds of spousal abuse, and the list continues.

No sect of society has been exempt, however, as custom rules, dictates, or governs our lives, we fall prey to denial..."there's no violence in my family."

Sadly, we seek, desperately, options that exercise our "pass the buck" theory. It works quite well...when situations and circumstances occur in life that perplex or provoke, alter or inconvenience our lives, our daily routines, we respond in some sort of violence. Be it physical, mental, sexual, or other, the result is the same...a death. When one person, incited to violence, acts out on another, he or she, whom the action has been taken against, will surely feel the consequences of such an attack, causing that person to die either physically, or spiritually. In either case, death has occurred.

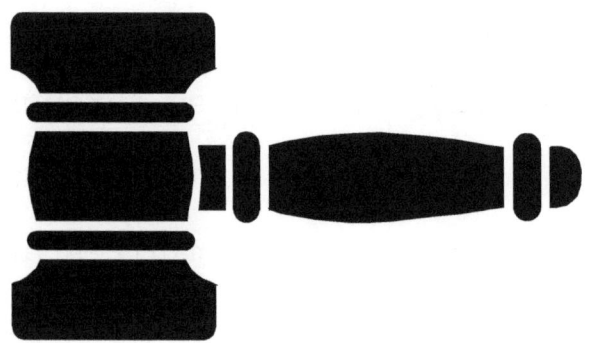

It's easy to say the spiritual death is the lesser of the two, yet I contend that it is not. For it is through this spiritual death, that pain and retaliation take place, usually on others. Thus creating a cyclical, and somewhat spontaneous event which may or may not be stopped. This cycle is manifested, if the individual is not rooted correctly, in homes throughout America in the form of family violence. It's manifestation equates to death...the destruction of a people.

When the Israelite, Jacob, lead his people to Egypt, no slavery existed among them. Yet, when their number began to swell, their security, so thought the Egyptians, became endangered for they knew this people belonged to the Lord. Thereafter came a king who because of this fear, oppressed these people.

If I enslave a people to fear, the people cease to be powerful...fear rules them and they become irrational and pragmatic, which leads to poor planning and poor decision making.

Fear serves as a tool to capture you hearts and minds, rendering you virtually inept. Vision becomes distorted, and direction is hindered from any progress; regression begins.

If we are a people of change and struggle, sacrifice and faith, I can see little sign of it.

The problem, then, is foundational. If one wishes to build a house, what does he do first? First, the land is prepared to support and accept the foundation which it is meant to hold. Second, the foundation itself is prepared, using the best materials (if it is to be made right), then mixed and poured into it's mold, and left to harden. Lastly, a structure is built. The same is true for us, there is a preparation period that must take place prior to any foundation pouring, or the building of any structure. Let us go back to our foundations and examine them well, for in them we are surely to find faults.

The Word of God is to be our foundation on which every part of our life must rest and reside. It is our anchor, created to hold us in place so God can do His perfect work both in and around us. Fear sets us in a vain of carelessness and cautious anxiety. The thought of the unknown perplexes and perpetuates our desire to "flee from" problems, persecution and pain. In our fleeting, panic overtakes and leads our hearts (just as a Shepard leads his flock of sheep) to make irrational and unreasonable choices, yielding in unwanted outcomes. Floundering in our frustration and failure, we seek remedies to soothe our aching hearts. Sexual promiscuity, solitude, suffering and shame become regular and routine practices. These devices, used to mask us from one another, backfire continuously, causing relational hurt between spouses, friends and families. Seeking amelioration, we turn to God in prayer (asking for forgiveness). We turn to Him as one looks to a lawyer for hired advice or representation. We go to God for help and resolution to our turbulent and troubled lives.

Turning our perspective to temporal things, we become selfish about our relationship with God. The Lord wants our pilgrimage, with him, to be one of a personal and loving nature, not one of demands. If the source of our strength be made known, let them know that it's roots originate with realizing a real and relevant relationship with God. Through cultivating this relationship; tending to it's every need, one may be able, then, to experience the joy and permanent peace of the Lord. Paul writes in his letter to Philippi, "Rejoice in the Lord always. I will say it again: Rejoice! Let your gentleness be evident to all. The Lord is near. Do not be anxious about anything, but in everything, by prayer and petition, with thanksgiving, present your requests to God. And the peace of God, which transcends all understanding, will guard your hearts and minds in Christ Jesus." Philippians 4:4-7 Being a participant in a relationship with the Lord entitles you to these benefits. One is then able to know God and His ways...His character.

Relationships, therefore, exist on a foundation not of selfishness and solitude, but of humility and servitude. This is the essence of things past, present, and future. Upon servitude, respect, adoration, and love for one another may be established. Each person seeking to meet the other's needs, relationships are formulated on a firm foundation on which strength may be realized through trust and love for one another.

There is a strong correlation between our worship and relationships with others. The manner in which we engage Worship typifies our commitment level to people in our lives,

God included. Worship requires certain things in order to be successful. Commitment, sacrifice, trust, to name a few, are all needed and necessary ingredients to any worship. Likewise, personal relations carry these same essentials.

Abraham, Isaac, and Jacob's, roots (or knowledge of God's person) ran deep. Illustrated throughout Genesis, these men had real relationships with the Lord. When God told Abraham to go up to the mountain with his son, Isaac, and two servants to make a sacrifice, he did as God instructed, believing that God would keep his promise of providing a sacrifice (besides Isaac). It was during the act of sacrificing his son (to provide atonement; the remission of sin by the shedding of blood), (note the symbolism) that God's angel called out to Abraham saying,"...Lay not thine hand upon the lad, neither do thy any thing unto him: for now I know that thou fearest God, seeing thou hast not withheld thy son, from me." Genesis 22:12

The act of sacrificing one's child is in fact divination.

Abraham, without the complete Word of God, knew the Character of the Lord. Abraham trusted that the Lord would provide a suitable sacrifice, for the Word says, "He (Manasseh, King of Judah) sacrificed his sons in the fire in the Valley of Ben Hinnom, practiced sorcery, divination and witchcraft, and consulted mediums and spiritists.

He did much evil in the eyes of the Lord, provoking him to anger." 2Chornicles 33:6

Somehow, we have replaced the promises of God; his plan and purpose for our lives have been skewed. They have been and are currently being misinterpreted. Disseminated throughout society carrying a different meaning, we, as a people have lost our significance to life...where is our purpose? Relationships have replaced the chains of yesterday, shackling us, yet keeping our people apart. Relationships, today, replaced slave ships of yesterday. Carrying it's poisonous values from one to another and from generation to generation, we kill, one another. We die by our own hand. Senselessly.

xxiv

*Let it Rain*

## Cacophony

The sadness which surrounds my heart is deep and rich with anguish. I am, as it were, troubled by the pride of man's heart. When I look at me, I see a figure full of selfish indignation; full of hatred and fear. Freedom is within his grasp, but because of pride, he grasps it not. He concedes to no one, and lacks all that could make him free. This man is slave to desires he cannot perceive or control. His enemy, himself,

*Rev. Christopher S. Times*

cascades a cacophony of gestures for him to utilize to perpetuate this fictitious life. This façade he calls home, captivates, and caresses his spirit. Even unto subtle submission, he falls freely to freedoms he does not hold. Deep within himself, boldness concurs his spirit, and pride puffs his head to an early, untimely grave.

This is the simple tragedy of me; of man. He falls to freedom not his own. He is his own enemy, capturing, and

*Let*

controlling that which G

to be. Pride before freedu

this the key? Surely not for me?

To see myself, and know what lies ahead is difficult, and nearly impossible. However, I believe that in order to do that which we were created, each of us must release and relent these things that vex us so honestly. To deny an untimely demise, my eyes must see the real me.

I feel my heart beating under my clothes, and wait for the sound of my birth. I chose to be born again! That I might serve

*v. Christopher S. Times*

the Lord, and not my selfish, hellish desires which serve only to imprison me. To captivate my spirit, and render my heart dead. I need life to live in me. My soul calls for me. It seeks my every need, and saturates my eyes with somber tears of sadness. They cry for me; for my lost soul comforts no one, not even thee. I am tired and weary. I am chained by shackles I cannot see. God, hold my hand and touch my feet. Free me, my spirit, so that I may reach eternity. I need thee to answer me. Touch my heart, that in its

*Let it Rain*

beating, it may bleed for me. My soul is touched by the palm of your hand. With your touch, heal me. Keep this broken heart alive in thy Spirit. Free my heart today, I pray. I am a proud man, filled with sorrow, and laced in greed. Teach me, O Lord to pray…

*Rev. Christopher S. Times*

## Clarity

I hear the trees as they bend
and bow against the whistling
wind.

I hear the songs that birds
often sing,
And meditate on the melodious
melody which proceed from them.

I see the sun's rays in silent
skies, and witness their
brilliance as they dance across
the waters.


I see raindrops as they fall
from flooded skies, as they fall

*Let it Rain*

from heaven, and touch my face
against the earth.

My feet, they feel heavy

When I sleep, they slumber

When I am tired, they carry me

When my mind breaks,

And I am afraid,

When I feel alone

It is they who lead my broken
spirit safely home.

Touch me.

Take my hand, and feel the sun
rise on my face.

Feel the winter winds blow

As I look to another day,

I pray.

*Rev. Christopher S. Times*

Silence my heart, and keep me
from the ground.

Take this lead from me,

For my hands are heavy indeed.


Carry me across the waters

And lay my mind at rest.

Speak peace to my soul,

That in my midnights

I may find Clarity.

*Let it Rain*

## Cacophony

The sadness which surrounds my heart is deep and rich with anguish. I am, as it were, troubled by the pride of man's heart. When I look at me, I see a figure full of selfish indignation; full of hatred and fear. Freedom is within his grasp, but because of pride, he grasps it not. He concedes to no one, and lacks all that could make him free. This man is slave to desires he cannot perceive or control. His enemy, himself, cascades a cacophony of gestures

*Rev. Christopher S. Times*

for him to utilize to perpetuate this fictitious life. This façade he calls home, captivates, and caresses his spirit. Even unto subtle submission, he falls freely to freedoms he does not hold. Deep within himself, boldness concurs his spirit, and pride puffs his head to an early, untimely grave.

This is the simple tragedy of me; of man. He falls to freedom not his own. He is his own enemy, capturing, and controlling that which God made

*Let it Rain*

to be. Pride before freedom? Is this the key? Surely not for me?

To see myself, and know what lies ahead is difficult, and nearly impossible. However, I believe that in order to do that which we were created, each of us must release and relent these things that vex us so honestly. To deny an untimely demise, my eyes must see the real me.

I feel my heart beating under my clothes, and wait for the sound of my birth. I chose to be born again! That I might serve the Lord, and not my selfish,

*Rev. Christopher S. Times*

hellish desires which serve only to imprison me. To captivate my spirit, and render my heart dead. I need life to live in me. My soul calls for me. It seeks my every need, and saturates my eyes with somber tears of sadness. They cry for me; for my lost soul comforts no one, not even thee. I am tired and weary. I am chained by shackles I cannot see. God, hold my hand and touch my feet. Free me, my spirit, so that I may reach eternity. I need thee to answer me. Touch my heart, that in its beating, it may bleed for me. My

*Let it Rain*

soul is touched by the palm of your hand. With your touch, heal me. Keep this broken heart alive in thy Spirit. Free my heart today, I pray. I am a proud man, filled with sorrow, and laced in greed. Teach me, O Lord to pray...

*Rev. Christopher S. Times*

## Negro Male

The destruction and corruption of the African-American Negro Male originates from his parents, primarily, however, the mother. In the home, she sets the standard. It is by her cadence that all occupants march. The proverbial "buck" stops with her. God has blessed her with wisdom and strength; when directed right, and nourished correctly, she can be an awesome motivator, lawmaker, and critic, all in one. It is her duty, therefore, to place

*Let it Rain*

the things of the Lord in his head and in his heart and hands. She should submit her family to God through much prayer and supplication. It is her heavenly assignment (while on Earth) to grow her children in such a way that they will respect, honor, and give to each other freely and be kind and courteous to everyone.

This destruction is like that of a cancer. It, from birth, is both small and non-obtrusive. When it matures, however, the cancer grows to an enormous

*Rev. Christopher S. Times*

size, killing and consuming all that is in it's path. As is the case with the Young African-American Male. The end is the same...a death. Of the hope I once had for this man, I hold no more. I can't count the tears I've shed for him. The wasted mind, and lethargic intellect grows deep in these hearts. It's seed rests deeply in every heart of these, and seeks to rest there, perpetually. Each seed gives way to new root, and each new root couples and grabs at the soul of us-desperately seeking vengeance on it's

*Let it Rain*

rooters lackadaisical behavior. Pride and anger ripples through and all that remains is the fear of being discovered.

The fear of losing what is left of us-we seek solace, but solace finds us not. Moment by moment, we seek our face-our minds melt into one bland reality. We tease, and rape ourselves of all that was once pure for the sake of something old-for something new. We laugh a dead man's laugh in hopes to raise ourselves, but there is no salvation in this...no amount of

*Rev. Christopher S. Times*

sacrifice can raise us from this deadened state. We lay here, unconscious and without life. Breathing the toxic fumes of years present and years past; I pray my way past this trap of societal and parental neglect. Things have become definitely difficult in this desperate day of deception and disdain.

Death; can I hear your sweet voice sour the sound of everything I hear? Could you laugh with me for just a little while? Can you hear my heart racing through you? Do you feel

*Let it Rain*

me in your arms, calling your name?

Have mercy on me!

My soul cries for thee, endlessly. Hold my heart in your hands. Give me my life, that I might see eternity. Let my eyes cast across the sea, and capture my hope-my bride to be. Let me live again, with sweet expressions of love and joy. Bury then deep within me, that in my haste, I might not forget.

I pray that my life finds meaning. That it fills with the light of my youth. May days, it

*Rev. Christopher S. Times*

seems, grow dark with sadness, and I find myself running.

Plant my feet where I may not fall. Keep me in your ear so that if I fail, or falter, I will always see my way through. Keep my heart, that the setting sun might fall on me, and bring me life!

*Let it*

## Potter's House

How can I hold my heart in my hand and not keep that that has kept me safe thus far?

How can I look to tomorrow?

How can I see it's shiny face?

Hold me in your arms, and let me fear nothing. Keep me still until this day is done; until I am safe again in you.

Allow my heart time to tingle with the loss of my yesterday.

Allow the grief of this to grieve me until I can bleed no more...

*Rev. Christopher S. Times*

Take my hands, and beat them;

Break them today-tomorrow.

Make them over, perfectly.

Enable them to speak truth to my

heart, and capture my mind so

that the good things come

through.

Leap into my life.

Be of the courage which rests

within me.

Bless my lips, that the lies I

tell will tell me that I am

free. I am free to be my

iniquity.

*Let it Rain*

Capture this heart of mine and see it clearly. Coax it to tell you my life.

Breathe into me the breath that I crave,

That life may be in me, and I might be restored

To longevity.

Free me.

My hands must talk.

They must speak again...

They must tell me my hopes

Tomorrow.

Breathe on my hands

That I may be glad.

*Rev. Christopher S. Times*

Make me over

So I may see again.

*Let it Rain*

## Preacher's Dream

If I could,

I'd fly away

In search of something lost

yesterday.


If I could,

I'd surely would

Find a way to capture lost

dreams.


If I could,

I'd tune my vision to see my

way free of life's tragedy,

*Rev. Christopher S. Times*

And take time to care for those who can't seem to find their way.


If I could only be all that I ever dreamed,

If I could just fill one desire I'd gladly do it.

*Let it Rain*

## Rain Fall

Fall Rain Fall

Down my windowsill,

When wet,

When dry

I know not why

The rain fall down my window.

That I might see still

To    know    that    I    might    be

knowledgeable in your ways

To feel the rain on my face,

The again falls down on me.

*Rev. Christopher S. Times*

## Serenity

Grant me eyes to see, O'Lord, that I might know thy perfect will.

Grant me humility, so I might serve with an open heart.

Grant me wisdom, so I might know that I might be, and become.

Grant me, Lord, understanding, so I might be able to understand that thy Word is my strength, my source is in thee.

*Let it Rain*

Teach me to love,

So I might love; for God is Love.

Lord, grant me peace; that I might have in me what is lacking...Serenity.

*Christopher S. Times*

# Friendship

Starting my life over again, I've come to know no one. It was said that if you were to avail yourself to be a friend, friends would intern, avail themselves to you. Then friendship, or any relationship, for that matter, is two way. If this is true, then, let time take hold-time will tell the difference. Giving, I've heard, comes from the heart. In the heart, and from it flows life in abundance. In my giving, I shall receive love-so it is thought-so it is.

*Let it Rain*

From my love, from my heart in all honesty, in all humility, I send to you my great desire. As do we all need, as do we all know of love, we obtain it only to keep. And in our hoping, we lose extremely. To give love is to obtain it in order to give it again to someone else.

In my living, I'd hoped to do one thing; give of myself until there is nothing left. If friendship is a two way street, I'll travel it, sharing my problems as well as yours, fears, plans, and ideas alike.

*Rev. Christopher S. Times*

Friendship is truly built on a foundation of trust.

*Let it Rain*

## Morning Dew

In the morning

I follow the rain,

That my tear-lit eyes might
find the morning dew.

I follow it well.


In the morning,

Life blooms

Buds of joy I see all over

Green and bright.

Life touches me in a simple
way

Words of wisdom do I hear,


Sounds of joy do I dance to,

I dance

*Rev. Christopher S. Times*

Sing do I to these that the morning brings

I follow it well.

I dance to the morning.

*Let it Rain*

## Meadows Green

Sometimes, I sing about the stone grass that perch in the meadows green. They seem to me to be simple and gray, yet with small gestures, carved memories remind me of them, and of who they were. I feel carefully cautious about lying there with them, seeing their early maze at sunlight.

Each day that the sun sets, my eyes fill with silent tears of saddened joy. I hold up my hand to the East to watch the sun

*Rev. Christopher S. Times*

fall. It falls, timely, on me,
and for a moment, the stone
grass glimmers like windowed
light.

*Let it Rain*

## Love

Love is a verb. It, by it's very meaning, denotes action. Love performs, persuades, and perfects our (spirits) hearts and minds to provide an unbelievable posture on which we can, and should promote this professing faith.

When we place our lips together, our tongue, and muscles, in that region of our jaw work in concert to perfect, and perform a symphonious sound called speech. This speech, we

*Rev. Christopher S. Times*

often take for granted, compels that that it is acted on to conform to some command or set of commands on queue. This ability to accomplish this was demonstrated when Jesus told Lazarus to come forth from the dead, and when Jesus called a prayer service, and the food was scarce, He called on the bread, and told it to multiply, and it did. He called on the fish, and told the fish to replicate itself a multitude of times, and it obeyed. Jesus calmed the angry sea with a whisper. He called out demons, and healed

*Let it Rain*

the sick with only a word. He is awesomely Awesome!

God taught us to consider things that were not as though they were. He is able to draw out of the darkest part of our lives, sunshine. He keeps us, and bears each burden we carry as his own. Therefore, this love of which we speak, is sacrificial. The Bible says that God so loved us that He gave his only son, Jesus, to us as a living sacrifice (which was paid on Calvery), that all past, present, and future sins of this

*Rev. Christopher S. Times*

world would be borne and put away forever. God's love is sacrificial. Love has professing power, protecting power, and replenishing power. When we speak with our lips, the promises of God, healing often takes place. The guidance of the Holy Spirit counsels, corrects, and cajoles us to conform the saved to safety. And finally, this restorative power replenishes continually. No matter how you give, or what you give, love never runs out. God's reservoirs of love are deep with grace, and kindness. They can

*Let it Ra_*

never be exhausted. This inexhaustible supply is everlasting! It is as deep and rich as the cycle of life.

If we are able to stand, let us stand for righteousness; that in our standing, we might profess; and in professing we may call; and in our calling, we might allow our hearts the privilege of confession. That in this, God's glorious grace might fall fully on us…

## Destiny

Deep inside the recesses of my mind, I see myself.

Dancing on willow weeds, I call myself away. Come to me, come to me , call upon my dreams, to be. Fall on me and follow the winding trail to this destiny. Follow me, and find my majesty. Follow me I pray.

On my memories, I find my resting place. It holds me here teasing and scolding these memories today. Talk to my hands and hew out their dignity.

*Let it Rain*

Couple them in this hollowed and heavy heart. Teach them to beat my chest, and with open palms breathe again. Bring life to these deadened scabs which rest on my finger tips. Hull out my heavy hands that in your hulling, they might not disappoint or confuse. Touch them. Make them real again. Make my life feel again like on yesterday.

To these eyes, Let them see again the reality they once possessed. Cast them across solid skies of gray, that in

*Rev. Christopher S. Times*

seeing, they might never lose sight of the pain which brought them. Keep them. Be them. See them, their loving arms embrace your tenderness. They engulf kindness on you and avail light unto the rainbows in your lives. Here! Take these arms and cast them. Make them and break them until they are no less than perfect. That in their perfected state, these arms might discover true perfection. Leap into my eyes that I may hear you. Your heart beating on my brokenness, my breast.

*Let it Rain*

Carry me away, today I pray

till I find another way to say,

I love you...

*Rev. Christopher S. Times*

## Nine Eleven

In a moment when time seems to stand still in both grief and despair, I hold my head and heart to the sound of Grace. For it is in this that we shall find sweet surrender and resolve toward a better tomorrow, today. I ponder on what makes men so mean and evil. The one issue comes to mind...need. The need to exercise ones power over another in the form of force compels us toward these societal evils, I believe. Engrossed in this, we cater to careless acts

*Let it Rain*

of violence which paralyzes and penalizes society as a whole, and individuals, in part.

I love America! I love the Land and the One who created both it and us. Jesus is the key to this senselessness. Salvation is at hand. Grasp it! Hold it! Cherish it!

*Rev. Christopher S. Times*

## I See The Sun

In my heart

I see the rain falling down on me,

It covers my soul till these arms of mine stretch

To feel the sun.


Rise, Rise

O' Sun, Shine on me

Light my life with the warmth of you.

Keep your arms around this heart of mine, that

In my living, I might not find

*Let it Rain*

No other resting place but thine.


Rise Sun Rise.

And fill these arms with your love,

That insodoing I might see the sun.

*Rev. Christopher S. Times*

## Youthful Memories

As I shed my youth

Silent gestures of simpler

times come to me.


I look over my arms to see

children play.

They dance in the sunshine

And the light reaches from

Heaven's Gate.


I look over to see raindrops;

I count them as they carefully

fall Earthward.

I see them as they dance

across silent sun-filled skies.

*Let it Rain*

I see the sun

Rising in the East

Blessing all who stands in its glory.


I look over toward the meadow, and meditate on

Melodious Melodies which reach across my face.

I see the sun.

The children

They run toward each other;

The air in full embrace.

Their arms tilted toward the sky,

Hands, filled with air.

*Rev. Christopher S. Times*

I look over

I see them dance across the water,

Eyes turned toward Heaven's Gates

Singing sweet songs of laughter.

I see the sun shining on their face.


Keep them

Meet them

Greet them

Teach them

These children of today.


I see the sun shining

*Let it Rain*

As rain falls from Heaven's Gate,

Touching the hands of those who I look over

To see dance amid silent skies in sunshine!

*Rev. Christopher S. Times*

## Bird Song

Now I hear the birds sing
their song;
Chime like a melody in my ear.

The rhymes they sing
Soothe the heart of me;
It moves that very part of me
Toward serenity
I see.

When sun lights rays touch the
morning due
I see you
Singing close to me.

*Let it Rain*

# Letting Go

I lost a friend on yesterday.

She broke my heart, then ran

away to stay.

I thought I could come her

way, but she frowned and went.


I lost a friend yesterday,

She came to play, and ran this

day

I thought I'd ask her to see

me,

Please me

Be me

By walking my way

*Rev. Christopher S. Times*

Instead, she turned her head
to say

Another day

Another way

I pray

She left me on yesterday.

*Let it Rain*

## Like Me

I wonder what it means to be
Black like me
To rap like me,
To tap like me

Is it fair?
I often wonder
Is it real to taste that
thrill?
To magnify my color, and hope
that the rain washes it off
By morning

*Rev. Christopher S. Times*

Lest the light captures you,
and sends down it's rays to tell
you
  Of your sins.


  Is it right for me to be
  Whatever I want
  When I want and where I want
  How I want?
  Can this be?
  For me?


  I wonder what it would mean to
be
  Black like me?


  Standing here

*Let it Rain*

Seeing eternity.

When the winds blow

And streams flow

And flowers break their doom

With their bloom

Will, then, it be

Ok to be Black like me?

*Rev. Christopher S. Times*

## Birds

In my mind there's a song I
hear,
It rises in the morning
To greet me.

On borrowed skies,
In distant eyes
I find it's keeping,
It follows me.

Against the waters
It glides and bribes my spirit
To feel another day
This way

*Let it Rain*

This May,

Summer skies fill me.


Ripe with the spice of life

I come to see you singing,

I hear you springing into a

Beautiful rhythm.

That a way

This a way

I hear you say on branches,

Sing your song

Till the morning comes

And touch a simple guy like

me.

*Rev. Christopher S. Times*

## Sorrowed Skies

Sorrowed, sorrowed skies that leap into my heart today. I see the sun shining against your face as to say good day.

I miss the ravens as they seek to peak into these eyes of mine. This pride of mine concurs my every move. Oh peace, come quickly. Be me, that dread which seeks me. Flee me. Be me. Free me. Keep me. My arms are heave with sorrow, and I look to the sun to calm my day.

*Let it Rain*

The breeze, it flows through me like a cool summer stream. Lap against these shores of mine, and rake away my demise this time. Break these bonds which hold me, that in my freedom, I might be free. Kiss my lips as the day dawns. Hold my hand till it folds. Break away this pain, I pray, that I may lose my self inside of you.

*Rev. Christopher S. Times*

## Eastern Skies

Eastern skies fill with silence
As I watch to tell of homecoming's own.

Eastern skies
Light my life with her memories,
Keep them safe within the recesses of my mind,
For in time when it comes,
I'll look to these to keep me
As the day goes by.

*Let it Rain*

Play with me,

Stay with me

Dip in the dawn that I see
your face.

Comfort this heart I embrace,

With the whispers of love

Which raised me.


Reach me

Teach me

To feel the evidence of your
life

as it passes me


I hold my hands to the somber
silent skies

In hope that in my reaching,

*Rev. Christopher S. Times*
Your arms might touch mine

Amid the Eastern skies.

*Let it Rain*

## K

Your smile brightens my life

Each time I see you

It shines as does the sun,

Giving hope and light in

Dark places.

Smile today

My sweet sunshine,

That your eyes might grant me

What I wish could be.

*Rev. Christopher S. Times*

## Remembering You


When I meet you, I saw you through my eyes, and found you beautiful.


How carefully you smiled at me

And considered what a blessing I'd be

To thee.

You held up my hands

And touched the very heart of me

While I labored to find my way clear

Of tragedy.

*Let it Rain*

My eyes held the image of you close,

And carried you with me till the end

My friend

My friend.

Just the thought of the sound of your voice

Captures and captivates my spirit.


With your eyes, You entangle me

With your lips, you encourage me

To be all God wants me to become.

*Rev. Christopher S. Times*

With the touch of your hand,

Marvelous memories blind, and

hold me close to you.


For through your eyes,

Love finds and forms the

deepest part of who I am.


When I see your face,

My knees

My heart

My eyes

Clatter with every breath.


I need you

To breath you

To see you

*Let it Rain*

To be you

For a little while.


Hold my arms around you,

And blow me that kiss

That I miss

That I miss


When I meet you,

I found the very start of you

The heart of you

I knew.


Remembering you...

*Rev. Christopher S. Times*

## I still remember your name


Waking up to see today,

I remembered your face.

You shinned at me

With sensitivity

Completely.


We danced

We sang

While rain drops fell around

us.


We laughed,

Time passed

And the wind

*Let it Rain*

Blew our hair in symphony.


I woke today,

And saw your face

In this place

I touched it with a smile.


While the waters rise in my

eyes

I cried this Time

Still,

I remembered your name.

*Rev. Christopher S. Times*

## Perfect Praise

In my praise,

I offer my hands to you

That they might be lifted in your will.


I give you my eyes,

That in blinded days

Among blind hours,

I might trace your heart.


Take these ears,

Make them into instruments of peace and praise.

That in my hearing,

*Let it Rain*

I might love and serve you

Truthfully.


From my lips,

Form words of wisdom

Which would walk with me

For eternity.

Use me.

Rev. Christopher S. Times

# About the Author

I attended public schools in Houston Texas as a child and began writing while in the tenth grade at Charles Milby Sr. High. While in College at Prairie View A&M University, my writing ability grew and I expanded and changed my writing style to include spiritual aspects of my life. Through my good and bad times, God has allowed me to prosper. For that, I give thanks.

Today I am an associate minister at Jordan Grove MBC in Houston, Texas.

# Author Information

Reverend Christopher S. Times

7800 W. Airport Blvd.

Apt # 713

Houston, Texas 77071

Phone Number (713)721-5095

Email cst6228@yahoo.com

Wallstreetcst@aol.com

Lightning Source UK Ltd.
Milton Keynes UK
UKHW04f0006250818
327762UK00001B/11/P